KU-039-188

Do Make

The power of your own two hands.

James Otter

Book Co

For you, William.
Stick to what you enjoy, you'll end up doing something you love.

Published by
The Do Book Company 2020
Works in Progress Publishing Ltd
thedobook.co

Text © James Otter 2020
Photographs © Mat Arney 2020,
except pages 104–117
© James Otter 2020

The right of James Otter to be
identified as author of this work has
been asserted by him in accordance
with the Copyright, Designs and
Patents Act 1988

All rights reserved. No part of this
publication may be reproduced,
stored in or introduced to a retrieval
system, or transmitted in any form or
by any means (electronic, mechanical,
photocopying, recording or otherwise)
without the prior written permission of
the publisher. Requests for permission
should be sent to: info@thedobook.co

To find out more about our company,
books and authors, please visit
thedobook.co or follow us **@dobookco**

5% of our proceeds from the sale of
this book is given to The Do Lectures
to help it achieve its aim of making
positive change: **thedolectures.com**

Cover designed by James Victore
Book designed and set by Ratiotype

Printed and bound by OZGraf Print
on Munken, an FSC-certified paper

A CIP catalogue record for this book
is available from the British Library

ISBN 978-1-907974-86-1

10 9 8 7 6 5 4 3 2 1

1045
CORK
CITY
LIBRARIES
8383

Contents

Prologue

Hands, fingers, fingerprints. We all have our own unique conduit through which we connect to the physical world.

I feel the deepest connection to the earth when I'm walking beneath a rich, luscious woodland canopy and I run my hand over the topography of tree bark. Or when I'm surfing in the ocean engulfed by a beautifully dynamic energy, stroking my hands through the cold, salty, swirling water. Two awe-inspiring spaces that exist on our incredible planet, connected to each other and to me, through my senses, through my hands.

As a maker, taking a raw piece of timber through a creative process of physical change allows me to connect back to the earth, back to the ocean and back to myself. Through the act of making, we reawaken our hands and minds to reconnect with the beauty of the natural world around us. Making allows us to slow down, offers an opportunity to grow in confidence, and can lead to a deeper sense of purpose.

It is an instinctive and intrinsic part of all of us that many have lost touch with. We just need the support, encouragement and confidence to get started again.

You already have the tools you need to start making.

They're right in front of you.

Your hands.

With dextrous fingers, millions of nerve endings and incredible coordination, you have the power to manipulate things, move things, make things.

And making something might just change your life.

Making a surfboard changed mine.

Some years ago, I was working at a timber-framing company in rural England, just outside the M25. The wood dust from the Douglas fir trees we were using to build the frames filled the air, our noses and our lungs. The heavier shavings seemed to land inside my boots and get caught on my socks. I had itchy feet. It was a hot summer and I longed to be back by the sea with its refreshing breeze. I missed the smell. As a surfer, I missed the waves.

Back then, I subscribed to a magazine, *The Surfer's Path*. It afforded me an occasional glimpse of the ocean — just enough to keep my longing satiated. One issue was particularly fitting: 'The Wood Issue'. I read the articles and pored over the images so many times that the pages became dog-eared. I can't remember the exact moment but, at some point, it inspired me to find a way to make a surfboard out of wood. It was the first time I'd even considered what it would involve and I found myself asking: what would be the best timber to use? How would I create a strong yet light structure? How would it feel in the ocean? The excitement and anticipation was already pulling me back to the sea.

As I went into the final year of a degree entitled Designer Maker, I had already made the decision to spend the next nine months exploring, experimenting and pursuing the idea of designing and making a wooden surfboard. However, when I broached the idea with my course tutors, let's just say they were apprehensive, if not openly dismissive. It was understandable: I mean, a surfer making a surfboard? It was hardly a novel idea. Their main concern seemed to be that a surfboard would be difficult for them to pit against their current marking scheme, and I could be jeopardising a good degree grade. A piece of furniture, for example, is functional, yet it offers huge scope for creativity in how it is designed and constructed. There is more opportunity for the creative and development stages to be represented and assessed. I'm fairly sure my tutors weren't surfers so I wasn't convinced they could see how much design, detail and skill went into the vision, construction and shaping of a surfboard. But I wasn't there for an argument.

I took their comments on board and, instead, made some pieces of furniture that employed construction processes similar to those I'd need to use. The ultimate aim was to finish the year with one, maybe two surfboards ready for a splash in the sea. For me, this journey was bigger than getting the right grade. In discussing the final-year piece with my tutors, I had massively downplayed how sure I was that this was the direction that my life was going to take.

After fervent researching, months of testing techniques and a serious amount of tea drinking, I finally had a surfboard sitting in my student bedroom. It was constructed out of 42 pieces of sweet-smelling cedar from Cornwall. Now it just needed shaping. I picked up my brass Lie-Nielsen block plane that I had treated myself to for my eighteenth birthday, checked the direction of the grain in the timber along the rail and pushed.

Have you ever experienced a moment in your life that you knew was shaping your future? The excitement, the anticipation, the connection was undeniable. I was in love.

In that moment, I knew. Regardless of anything and everything else in my life, I had to keep doing this: I had to keep making wooden surfboards. Making this board had changed my life.

Before we get started, it seems worthwhile to define the world of making as I know it. Of course, there are many different forms of 'making' and much of what I write about will still be applicable to them — acting, singing, composing music, cooking, drawing, painting, ceramics, the list goes on. However, this book will relate predominantly to the world that I inhabit, as a maker who works almost exclusively with wood. Over time I have come to define making as:

The act of taking a material and physically changing its state and/or shape to create something new that has a specific use or purpose.

It spans the world of art *and* craft. Making encompasses them both.

In writing this book, my hope is to rekindle the joy of working with your hands regardless of the medium that you choose to work in — and to explore the benefits that this 'maker space' provides. It will be a journey of discovery and connection. Along the way I'll share some of my reflections of where this reconnection to our hands can lead.

We'll begin with an understanding that making and creating are fundamental to us all. How our hands are a conduit that allows us to connect to the physical world around us. We'll define a process of making that can work for us all, and learn how the most important thing is simply to rely on and trust in that process. Finally, we'll look at the most powerful and influential things that making has given to me, and will give to you. Namely, a connection back to the planet, back to other people and, ultimately, back to yourself.

PREPARATION

1
**We are all
born makers**

Every child is an artist.
The problem is how
to remain an artist
once they grow up.

—

Pablo Picasso

When was the last time you created something you were willing to put your name to? How far back do you have to go? Yesterday, last week, last year ... maybe even back to school? If you cast your mind back to your childhood, do you have memories of making and creating? Clicking Lego pieces together, digging your fingers into Play-Doh, or running them through paints and across pieces of paper?

When we are children, play and creation seem to fall hand-in-hand. Through play, we interact with the world around us and become aware of our own sense of uniqueness. The marks we make on a piece of paper with our fingers dipped in paint, the shapes we squeeze and mould out of dough and the structures we build by clicking blocks together have come to exist through us and our hands. In their own small way, they stand as a physical representation of how we have made our mark on the world around us. And as children, we have no problem presenting them to the world: 'Mum! Dad! Look what I made!'

Those early memories will almost always be connected to a person or people with whom the experience is shared —a parent, sibling, teacher or best friend. With these people, we are exploring our impact on the world, collaborating and interacting to create shared visions. They are also the people whose judgement ultimately has the strongest impact on what we decide to do next.

The reason we all struggle to remain artists as we grow up is that we learn to fear judgement. We get caught up in trying to create something that's perfect, so it isn't judged negatively. At school, especially, when we start to compare our creations with those of our friends, we begin to believe the story that maybe we aren't quite good enough. That perhaps our talents lie elsewhere. So gradually we stop creating. We stop making.

In order to create and make again, we need to understand how to release ourselves from the judgement of others and, more importantly, of ourselves. We need to see that the pursuit of perfection is not a healthy one. We must recognise the story that we are telling ourselves — the one we are now living — and work out how that needs to change in order for us to believe that we *can* do things. We *can* be creative. We *can* make things.

The idea of craftsmanship is to continually work on a process, seeking perfection through a feedback loop that requires judgement from yourself, while acknowledging that true perfection is unattainable. So craftsmanship is a celebration of judgement and an intrinsic understanding that things will be 'wrong', yet we do them anyway.

Anthropologist Alice Roberts once said that we humans are thinkers and makers and those two things combine uniquely in our species.

For me, the two things are inextricably linked. The act of making, actively using our hands, gives us the opportunity to think. It creates a point of focus for the conscious mind and the physical body that allows space for the subconscious mind to wander, much like in meditation. As a result, it is recognised as a process that can be used for therapeutic purposes. In fact, the practice of occupational therapy was born from the Arts and Crafts Movement of the late nineteenth century, which actively promoted a return to handcrafting as a response to industrialised production.

Yet here we are, almost 150 years later, and as a society we are even more disconnected from our hands, from materials and from the earth. However, the connection isn't completely lost. Creativity is very much all around us. More than likely you are practising it already.

Do you remember the last time you tried a new recipe, when you cracked open a favourite cookbook and thumbed your way through its pages until something jumped out that you wanted to try and recreate? You followed the instructions as best you could, step by step, likely adding your own twist by replacing an ingredient with something you actually had in the cupboard. Smelling and tasting it as you went to try to get a sense of where the dish was headed. You tried to wrap your tongue and taste buds around the flavours that are being filtered through your senses until, excitedly and nervously, you dished it out onto a plate.

As you ate, weren't you often wondering if it might have been a little more tender if you'd taken it off the heat sooner, or maybe the sauce would have been richer in flavour and texture if you'd left it to simmer for a few more minutes? Whatever happened, you'll either have created a delicious meal and discovered new ingredients and a process that you will replicate another time, or accepted it's not the best thing you've ever eaten and you'll look to find ways to improve it next time. Whatever the outcome, you gave it a go and most likely learned something to enrich your understanding.

> Humans do two things that make us unique from all other animals: we use tools and we tell stories. When you make something, you're doing both at once.

Adam Savage

Working with raw materials to produce something that didn't exist before, in this case ingredients to create a meal, is a form of making that most of us engage in on a daily basis. Taking those materials through a process that delivers a desirable outcome may seem basic, but it can be incredibly rewarding. If the headspace and sense of satisfaction that cooking gives us can be celebrated and enjoyed, making something — *anything* — will benefit our mood. In fact, engaging in this kind of meaningful, practical activity is not only of benefit, but essential to good mental health, and making doesn't need to stop at the morning cup of coffee or the evening meal.

Now more than ever, as a society — as human beings — we need to recognise the physical and mental benefits of making, and support and encourage each other to give it greater prominence in our lives, and create time for regular practice.

When we were children, making came naturally. All we need is the space, encouragement and confidence to get started again.

2

What to make

We are born makers.
We move what we're learning
from our heads to our hearts
through our hands.

—

Brené Brown

When I think back over my own maker journey, from early memories of shaping clay in art classes and working on different wood joints in the school workshops, I realise that there were always two purposes or drivers for my outcomes. Some of the time, it was simply a case of trying to wrap my mind around a physical change: experimenting, learning, making for the sake of making. The rest of the time was spent thinking about the final outcome of the object I was making. What was its function, use or purpose in the world once finished?

For me, this is the point at which I draw a line. The difference between a 'craftsperson' and an 'artist'. Both are creative endeavours, both involve making, but there is a subtle difference. For me, a craftsperson is creating something that has a physical function or use; it is the world of 'craft'. Function over form. An object is created to follow an intended, or designed, outcome, whereas an artist is creating to experiment and explore processes that result in an outcome that can tell a story, and be appreciated visually or physically. It is where form often comes before function. I must stress that the line is often blurred and there is nothing to say that a maker cannot be both artist *and* craftsperson. This is simply how I have come to distinguish the two pursuits.

This really became apparent when a friend, Ben Cook, joined me in the workshop to make his own surfboard. As a professional artist, he was keen to use the surfboard to experiment with some mark-making towards the end of the process. The plan was to practise a technique known as *shou-sugi-ban*, where you char the surface of timber using a naked flame to light the wood, but you then let it go out before it starts to burn. Not only does it look good, turning the charred timber to black, but it can also make the board more weatherproof. Obviously, after spending five days making a surfboard, it can be quite risky! Fortunately, I had some experience of using the technique so I was able to calm his nerves as we lit the blow torch. Ben's plan was to char the tail of the board and fade the burning all the way to the nose.

The designer in me immediately envisaged a perfect gradient of colour, from the blackest black at the tail, slowly and evenly fading until it was just the bare, untouched wood at the nose. After three or four rounds of the burning, it was apparent that the wood simply burned to different colours as you moved across the grain. It was going to take quite a lot of work to create a smooth gradient of colour. However, as I reached for the sandpaper to begin working back some of the darker areas of the board, Ben reached out and stopped me. He was happy with it. He considered it finished.

The artist in him loved the fact that the end result was an uneven and unique pattern of colour — a direct response to the natural material. He felt it was more honest to the process itself to leave it like this. The designer in me found it difficult to come to terms with how the outcome differed from our intended goal, but as it was his board, I stepped back and let him sign the board with his name and all of its perfectly imperfect markings. As I said, the line is blurry, but for me this experience brought into focus the sense of difference between the artist and craftsperson mindsets.

There is incredible beauty in simple and elegant design. The real gold comes when form and function align. The point at which we struggle to define something as either functional or beautiful is the pinnacle of great design.

> Form follows function —
> that has been misunderstood.
> Form and function should be one,
> joined in a spiritual union.
>
> —
>
> Frank Lloyd Wright

Recently, I spoke with friend and ceramicist Jake Boex about this. He creates hand-thrown vessels, such as cups, from local materials. Within the simplicity of what he is creating, he saw an opportunity. Could the cup itself, this simple, functional object, be a blank canvas on which to communicate a story?

'Take a cup, it's a functional object, and yet in that really simple object we find such a depth in the story of the material. The clay, the sediment and the glaze. Where have these different parts come from? We throw them together on a wheel to create a story about the earth and the environment and by making such a simple object as a cup, that we use every day, the story becomes more real, more vivid, and increases the opportunity for appreciation of the environment and the one finite planet that we live on. With my cups, I hope to inspire people to feel passionate about the earth so they cherish it, rather than scaring them in the way that environmentalists have done before.'

Jake dances along the line that I use to define an artist. His cups are undeniably functional, but he plays with their form to define a narrative, subtly guiding people back to the earth from where it all started. He is the perfect example of a maker exploring craft and art simultaneously.

I enjoy processes of creation and have always been drawn to creating in an artistic way, as I find it freeing and fun, but I take much deeper satisfaction from creating an object that has a functional use. It's why the 'maker' path I have pursued in a more focused and determined way has been that of becoming a craftsperson, and also why I've never quite felt the need to overcomplicate the design or decorate anything I make. For me, the simpler something can be, the better. It just so happens that when you make something out of wood, the beauty is often apparent without too much work. Just awareness and selection throughout the process.

The more we use an object, the more we value it, the more we cherish it, and therefore tend to look after it. This means it is likely to last longer, and this becomes more poignant when the memories we make while using the object are fond ones. So, when it comes to deciding *what* to make, I would encourage you to look at areas of your life that already bring you joy and opportunities for fond memories. As ceramicist Jono Smart writes: 'I want to make things that are used every day. Things that become part of daily routines and rituals. That become part of Sunday morning breakfasts, remind you of a friend, or get placed each night on a bedside table.'

Through regular use, an object is more likely to be cherished. Those are the objects I have always most enjoyed making, and it's a great place to start your making journey. For example, I like making furniture because of how it allows play, freedom and experimentation throughout the making process, but also tends to be very functional and is likely to be regularly used.

I enjoy working on larger projects with a team, like those summers spent at the timber-framing company, not only because of the connections made with the people you work alongside, and the sense of accomplishment as those projects come to a close, but also because those projects have so much meaning for the customers, whose daily lives will have a continual interaction with the space or structure we made.

But the deepest and strongest satisfaction comes when I am making something that I hope to have exciting, fun and thrilling experiences with. For me, this is why, when I made that first wooden surfboard, it resonated on so many different levels that I shaped the next decade of my life around it. In making surfboards, I have found something that I deeply enjoy, and I have always been guided by my father's simple advice: 'Stick to what you enjoy and you'll end up doing something you love.'

So, look at what excites or stimulates you as a person and then think about what you can make to enjoy those moments with. It could be making a cup to drink your tea from or if you have children in your life, you could think about making a simple toy for them. If you enjoy your time in the kitchen, making a spatula out of a piece of wood can be an easy project to start with. You'll only need a saw and a chisel or knife to shape it with. If you prefer the idea of working with softer materials, maybe look into how to make an item of clothing, or even start with a cushion cover. Take a look around you. You will see handmade items everywhere, which means there are many opportunities for you to make something that fits you and your lifestyle.

You never know where a journey of making may lead, but unless you take those first few steps, you'll never find out.

CORK
CITY
LIBRARIES

3

Reconnection to material

My house was once an acorn.

Roger Deakin

Once you have decided what to make, the question that inevitably follows is: 'What should I make it out of?'

For me it was a simple choice. I have always been drawn to woodlands. Staring up at the tree canopy as it sways in the wind, picking up sticks to test which ones break easily in my hands, which make good walking companions or will be best for playing 'fetch' with the dog. My connection to wood has always been there — and in my view, we're all intrinsically connected to it.

Despite wood being a natural material, when using it to make something, it is possible to do so with no connection back to the land. You can buy timber over the counter at your local builders' merchant with no idea of where and how that timber has been grown, harvested and processed. Just because a material is natural, it doesn't mean it's sustainable or environmentally friendly. You can ensure that the timber you use has come from a well-managed forest. In the UK, it's the FSC — Forest Stewardship Council — certification that you're looking for. But even then, it doesn't cover the whole of the supply chain. For example, the retailer selling it doesn't have to be certified themselves. So, for me, having such a personal connection to wood as both a living organism and a material to make beautiful, functional objects, it seems sensible to understand the woodland management and forestry values of the timber that I use. For this reason, I work directly with the foresters who harvest our timber, so we know exactly how the woodlands are being managed and that the people on the ground are doing their best to be stewards of the land itself.

My grandad was a farmer in Wiltshire and 'stewardship of the land' is a phrase that I came across in one of his journals. It's the idea that we are never owners of land, nothing is ever 'ours'. All we ever do is borrow it for the short time we are on this planet, and then pass it on to future generations. I would like to think that my impact on this world will be a positive one for the generations that follow me. Understanding this position, where we nurture and care for the land we live on and use, is fundamental to that. With global trade that infuses all of our lives, the effect that we, as individuals, have on the planet is truly incomprehensible. But with everything I make, I do my utmost to ensure that it is completely traceable and has the lowest negative impact possible.

> Everything we personally own that's made, sold, shipped, stored, cleaned and ultimately thrown away does some environmental harm every step of the way, harm that we're either directly responsible for or is done on our behalf.
>
> Yvon Chouinard

There are a huge number of elements that factor into this equation, but for me the starting point is knowing exactly where our timber is grown and how it is managed to ensure the woodlands remain healthy and biodiverse in perpetuity. Every few months, I go to the woodland where our timber is harvested, and sometimes have the chance to witness a tree being felled.

Watching a living organism that has been growing on this planet — exchanging carbon dioxide for oxygen and creating a living habitat for thousands of other species — for anything from 20 to 80 years, being brought to the ground is a truly heart-stopping moment. In a matter of seconds its life comes to an end. The weight that falls to the ground is not only felt through the vibrations in the ground, but as a serious responsibility. Now, as the person who has created the demand, I must use as much of the tree as possible and make something worth making. It must be made to the best of my abilities and last as long as possible.

Of all the materials we use to make things — ceramics, metals, fabrics, plastics and wood being the most popular — for me, wood has the most tangible source. Along with ceramics and some fabrics, it is probably the most 'natural' of the materials, but the simple fact that trees seed, flourish and grow in the same kind of time frame as humans makes them far easier to connect with. Wood was an obvious choice when it came to selecting the material I was going to work with but, believe it or not, it was a choice that went against the norm.

A typical surfboard will be made from polyurethane foam, with an exterior shell of fibreglass and polyester resin. Not all surfboards are made this way, but it has been the industry standard since the surfing boom of the 1960s. Historically, all surfboards were made of wood, then in the 1920s a pioneer in surfboard design, Tom Blake, began to use plywood to adapt his surfboards and paddleboards. He began by drilling holes in solid wooden paddleboards and using a skin of plywood on the top and bottom to seal them up again. This made his boards much lighter; when he competed in paddle races, he ended up winning most of the time. This was the birth of the hollow wooden surfboard. He then went on to develop a construction process for making hollow boards that, in essence, is very similar to the way we make our boards today.

Unlike making surfboards from foam, using wood is not a quick process. Our typical board takes about 70 hours to make, from sawn planks through to finished board. Industry-standard foam boards can be made by hand in four to six hours, and machine-made in far less time. Foam surfboards suit the manufacturer: they are cheap and fast to produce, and aren't made with longevity in mind. In fact, in the professional world of surfing, the pursuit of higher performance led to surfboards being lighter, and in turn more fragile. Most pro surfers get through dozens of surfboards (if not more) per year, so when I first began making hollow wooden boards, I wondered if I could make one that was comparable in performance to a typical surfboard and could far outlast it.

One of the most overlooked characteristics of any product made today is longevity. How long is the product actually designed and made to last? And what can be done with it at the end of its 'useful' life? Fortunately, when we use natural materials, they can be left to decompose without harming the environment. The difficult part for us comes down to the adhesives and the finishes. Because we are trying to make something that is robust enough to endure years of use in the ocean, we have to compromise on the environmental impact of the materials used. It is something we are constantly assessing and trying to improve, but the guiding principle is that the lowest-impact product is likely to be the one that lasts the longest — and can be fixed and repaired indefinitely, which is where we currently sit.

All creative activities will have an impact on the world around us, and in order to move forwards, we have to start somewhere. If we accept that we were born creative beings, and we all ought to search for a way to express ourselves creatively, it would be best if these endeavours had as little environmental impact on the world as possible.

Once you have decided what to make, the material you're going to use and where you might source it, the question then is: how to get started?

PROCESS

4
Getting started

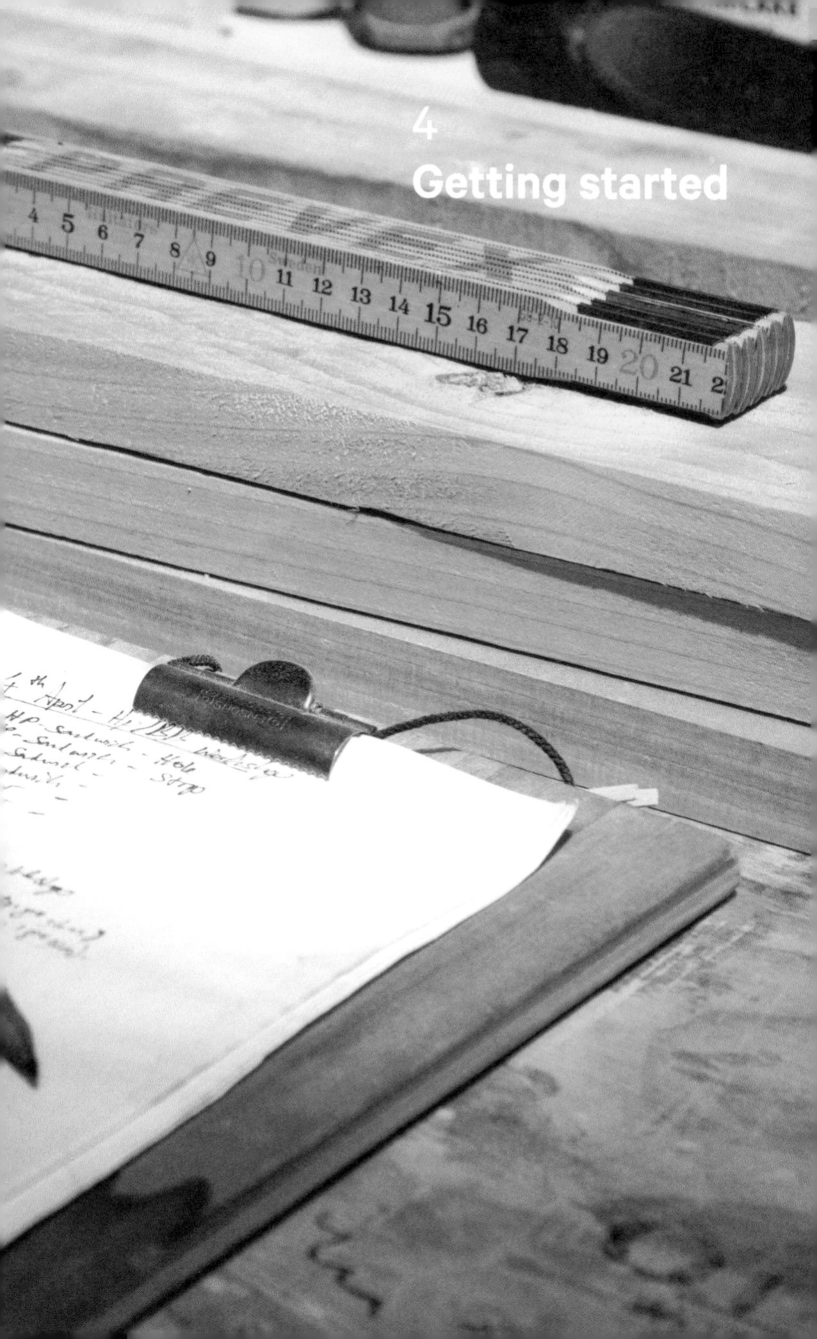

Creativity involves an incessant exchange between play and technical mastery.

Shaun McNiff

When it comes to getting started, the thought of what you're about to embark on may seem daunting. I still feel this way when we have tight deadlines, even though problem-solving and being pushed to try, test and learn new things is one of the most exciting elements of designing and making. But this doesn't mean that the prospect of starting a new project can't be a little overwhelming at times.

At these points, I find it helpful to be aware of the purpose behind what I am making. Understanding exactly why I want to bring this object into the world can help motivate me to get started.

Meaningful making

Whether you're making simply for the sake of making, or whether you have a purposeful outcome in mind, it is really helpful to understand exactly *why* you are making something. So, at the risk of sounding like Simon Sinek, let's start with why.

If it is simply for the pleasure of making, what do you

hope to gain from the experience? Do you want a deeper understanding of the materials you'll be working with, or is it a desire for a calmer state of mind from total absorption in a process? If your purpose is to make something with a specific use in mind, what problem does that object solve and is that compelling enough to take you all the way through the process?

There is literally no right or wrong way to answer these questions, but it will help if you clearly understand why you're doing it and what you want to achieve. Not only will that help you to get started, but it will keep you going as you reach tricky stages during the making process.

Moving out of your own way

Then we face the next challenge, and possibly the most common reason that many of us don't do things. It's the same reason most of us stop being creative or expressive in the first place: fear.

Fear of being judged, of not being good enough, of not knowing, of losing control, of being stuck. And, of course, a fear of failure.

If there's one thing I have learned through a lifetime spent making, it is this: failure is not an option.

Anyone who knows me will know that I'm not saying that in a macho, bullish, 'Big Boss' kind of way, but one where you understand that if you don't slip up and make a few mistakes, then you actually limit your scope for learning and developing a deeper understanding of the process or materials. So, you either end up making what you want to make with no trouble at all, or you face some problems along the way and learn from them. There is literally no way that you *can* fail. So why be fearful of it?

Image shows the anatomy of a surfboard with the framework glued onto the bottom skin, a solid tail block and thin strips running the length of the board along the rail.

Here is an example. When we make a surfboard, we start by fixing an internal framework onto a bottom skin (pictured). We then add rails — strips that are fixed to the framework and run along each side of the board. These rails are made by gluing 12 long, thin pieces of wood on top of each other, one at a time. To get them to follow the curvature of the outside of the board we need them to bend.

There is a very real limit to how much any one piece of wood can bend. And here's the tricky part: every single piece of wood will bend in its own unique way, and to its own unique limit. If you bend a piece of wood too far, guess what? It'll snap. Once a piece of wood snaps, there is absolutely no way you can fix it so that it behaves in the same way as before. Yes, you can glue it back together, but the strength and flexibility of the glue will be different from the wood itself, so whatever happens, it will be compromised somehow.

So, a crucial part of what we learn every single time we bend a piece of wood to fit onto the rail of a surfboard — that's 24 times for each board — is what wood looks, sounds and feels like as it bends. This is in the hope that we can bend each piece to the necessary amount without it snapping.

There are two processes we use to help us bend the wood more easily. First, we cut the timber to a profile that lends itself to bending; if you have a rectangular profiled piece of wood, it will bend much more easily perpendicular to its widest face as opposed to its shorter one. Therefore, a square piece of timber will bend in two directions evenly (assuming completely consistent grain direction and tightness), and a round piece of timber will bend evenly in every direction. So, for our rail strips, we make them as close to round as possible, but with a profile to allow them to join together easily. Still with me?

Secondly, we steam the wood, which softens the lignin (the protein that holds the stiff cellulose fibres together) and makes it more malleable. If we steam it too much, the wood becomes too easy to bend and actually kinks on each contact point of our framework; too little and the wood stays too stiff and snaps before reaching the framework at all.

While we have fine-tuned a process that will work 99 per cent of the time, there are always going to be anomalies, times when the rail strips just ... snap. We need to be vigilant in our observations so that we can recognise when it's about to happen. That way, we can apply more steam or simply choose a different rail strip. If the wood snaps as we fit it, there is a long delay while we let the glue we've applied dry before being able to clean it up and begin the process of attempting to fit another one in its place.

We know that each and every time we pick up a rail strip, that piece of timber may have a defect, flaw or quirk to its grain direction that will make it snap as we bend it. So every time we begin to bend it knowing full well that it may fail, but without trying, we would never learn what works and how far we can push the process.

How do you know what a stick looks, feels and sounds like when it's about to break, without breaking any sticks?

As my other grandfather used to say, 'If you don't make mistakes, you don't make nothin'.' And although it is incorrect use of English, he is emphasising the importance of making mistakes and failing. If everything always goes perfectly and no mistakes occur, what are you really gaining? It is in the brilliance of these failures that improvement, learning and progress happen.

So, when it comes to fear of failure being a reason why we don't do things, I would argue that, over time, the biggest sense of failure comes from not even trying in the first place.

Make space

Before you get started, clearing a physical space will be helpful. I am lucky enough to have regular and easy access to our workshop, which has all the space, materials and tools I need to start making. I find that the way we organise the space in the workshop can help or hinder our ability to get going.

Often, when you get stuck into making something, tools and other elements can get spread around the space you're working in. What feels natural to you might look incredibly chaotic to an observer! This is fine during the making process, but if you leave the space like this, it becomes a barrier for the next time and the opportunity to begin making something again diminishes rapidly. As a result, I find it really important to tidy everything away at the end of each session — this is especially crucial if you are sharing the space with others.

Over time, the small team in our workshop have organised the space so we know where each individual tool should be left. We have walls full of tools hanging on their own unique hooks with an outline drawn around the tools, so you know exactly which one is missing if you see a space with an empty silhouette. It may seem a little obsessive, but it's so much easier to complete any of our tasks when we know where tools are. We are far less likely to get distracted if we don't have to hunt for a particular tool and, in general, it tends to help bring a sense of calm when we're working in a tidy, ordered environment.

I'm the first to admit that I'm probably the worst person in our team for clearing up and putting everything away, but even I have my limits. There is often a point where I have to stop working and have a quick tidy-up to make sense of everything and allow the making to flow again.

Recently we've been doing some house renovations, so I've had a variety of tools that have moved around the house as the jobs have evolved, from wiring in electrics to fitting sinks, from plastering walls to hanging doors, fitting flooring, moving studwork and everything in between. Each task has needed specific tools and I would say that one of the most stressful parts of the job has been not knowing where a specific tool is — and I certainly noticed that morale on-site always improved if we had the chance to tidy up at the end of each day.

So, if you could dedicate a space in your home, garage or even garden shed that could be kept clear for you to make in, as and when you are able, that would be ideal. If that isn't possible, having the ability to clear a space where you won't be easily interrupted would be good too. Either way, you'll find getting started is much easier if you have a clear space with your materials and tools close to hand but in some kind of order. I know I do.

Clear your mind

As much as clearing a physical space will help you get started, clearing your mind is an equally useful skill to work on. It's the element of making that draws me back more than any other; in all honesty, I still don't quite know if I feel I need to clear my head to start making, or whether it's the making itself that helps clear my mind.

It is undeniable how meditative the making process can be. We become completely focused on the object that is in our own two hands, as we directly, or via tools, manipulate it into a new shape. Our conscious mind begins to quieten, our breathing and heart rate slow to a regular rhythm and our muscles begin to relax.

Even though I know this to be true, I find it easier to reach this place if I have taken a little time to declutter and calm my mind beforehand. You can get caught in your conscious mind for longer than necessary when making, and that can often lead to errors.

Thinking, 'I should really put the dishwasher on, so that everything is ready to cook dinner when my partner gets home. In fact, what are we even having for dinner?' can really interrupt your ability to focus. I personally find it best to do those little things, like putting the dishwasher on, first. Just be careful not to slide into a world of procrastination. Remind yourself of your purpose so that you come back to it and get started with excitement.

Practising a mindful approach to our thoughts can be really helpful. We don't know where they come from and we also know that we can't control them, so learning to recognise thoughts and let them pass without dwelling on them can be a great skill to master in order to calm your mind. Often, thoughts with absolutely no relation to anything can drift into my mind while I'm making something. Yet it is in this headspace that some 'eureka' moments occur. In fact, we have a phrase that we use in the workshop: 'Bandsaw Brainstorming'. The bandsaw is a piece of equipment that rips down long planks of wood. It seems to provide just the right level of focus and repetition that leads to thoughts of creativity, or answers to some of our unanswered problems, seeming to arrive out of nowhere.

When these thoughts come to mind, I'll often note them down or share them with someone in the workshop, before coming back to the present moment and the task in front of me. It's actually not too difficult to refocus when you have a loud and dangerous blade spinning a few inches from your hands, making its way through solid timber.

While it can be of enormous benefit to calm your mind before you start making, the most important thing is to just get into the making. Sometimes, if I'm feeling overwhelmed by the 'to do' list or the day-to-day of running a business and having a family, there is nothing better than picking up the plane and working the wood. The act of making can bring a sense of calm and space back into your life in much the same way that a physical activity like running or yoga, or a few minutes of mindful breathing or meditation can. As I said, sometimes creating a calm state of mind can help with making, while sometimes making can help create a calm state of mind.

> You can make any human activity into meditation simply by being completely with it.

Alan Watts

Dive in

To recap the steps to getting started: the first is to understand the purpose of what you're making. The second is to understand that whatever comes out of this session of making, it will provide an opportunity for learning and development. The third is to create a space, mentally and physically, so you can feel comfortable making.

Then, the final step: take a breath and dive in.

If you're excited by the thought of making something out of wood, then feel free to follow the step-by-step guide to making a handplane that can be found in the Appendix at the back of this book. If you're not familiar with a handplane, it is an object used when bodysurfing to increase the usable surface area of your hand to generate more lift, allowing your head and chest to come up from the water, in turn reducing your drag. It gives more speed and enables you to glide along waves far more easily.

It is possibly the simplest way to enjoy the thrill of being pushed along by the energy and power of the ocean and we surfers love it!

With your hands and a few simple tools, you can make something to have fun in the sea with. If a handplane is not for you, the guide can also be followed to make a bread board or a chopping board.

If finding a space at home and diving in on your own feels like too much of a challenge, you can find guidance to make almost anything online. YouTube is a great platform for amateur and professional makers to share their skills and processes. Failing that, when it comes to learning new skills nothing beats human interaction. Find out what part-time or evening courses are available locally, either in colleges or other maker spaces, and of course, you can join us in the workshop anytime.

5
Trust the process

> If you focus on the process of climbing,
> you'll end up on the summit.

Yvon Chouinard

Over the years of making surfboards and teaching others how to make them, I have found it incredibly helpful to have a process that I trust. Although each surfboard we make is unique in terms of its shape, the pieces of wood we use, and the hands that make it, the same process is applied to each.

I spent the first three years or so refining this process until the significance of the adjustments reduced and I had something that was robust enough to share with our customers. In truth, the refining never truly stops and, just like the act of making, we're always looking for ways to improve things next time around. I'd say I made about 15 surfboards before it felt like the necessary steps were becoming easier to replicate. There was still enough tolerance within the process to allow for the inevitable mistakes, but if I simply worked my way through step by step, I could make a surfboard that I was happy with. Happy enough to put my name to.

The idea of 'trusting the process' was popularised in the world of sports as an attitude to use to achieve long-term goals. In terms of making something, I find it helpful because it can be applied to your approach to things generally, or more specifically to exact tasks.

Broadly speaking, you might think about how to create something, try it and learn from any mistakes, then have another go until you manage to make what you set out to make. In other words, trial and error *is* the process.

In our workshop, when we worked alongside customers in the early days, it was easy enough to rely on my total absorption in the making process to ensure we followed everything step by step. We did this for the first couple of years, and luckily, no major mistakes were made! As the surfboard-making courses evolved and more people came through the doors, it became easier to get distracted. It felt like it was only a matter of time before a significant mistake was made. I was fearful that we would forget a key element in the making process, so I needed a formula. I started writing checklists for each stage.

I began by breaking down the whole process into small steps that included every single detail I could imagine. The smaller the steps and the more detail, the better. Of course, there were parts that I missed, so gradually I added them in, refining the process each time. Eventually I would use this as a 'playbook' to deliver the course. Having something fixed that you can rely on is incredibly freeing. It actually allows for the inevitable distractions, as you know you will always have the checklist to bring you back and guide you forwards.

It also provides a great framework of objectives to be reached by the end of each day, or each session. As our workshops are time-sensitive, it ensured that we remained on track to reach the end of the week with the desired result: a beautiful, *finished* surfboard.

If you work through the 'How to make a handplane' guide at the back of this book, you'll get a sense of the simple playbook we use for our handplane-making courses.

Of course, it doesn't capture all of the details that we have learned over the years, but it will help you make your first one. From there you can learn, iterate and find a process that works for you.

As we made more surfboards, inevitably, things would go wrong — rail strips would snap, skins would crack, joins would move — so we included adjustments to allow for these in the process. Having this basis of understanding means that each time we set out on the journey of making another board, we are actively looking for and noticing new things that can help to fine-tune the process further. In a funny way, this means that the more we make, the more detailed and refined the process becomes, even though it's the same one we've used for the past 10 years. The great thing is that the more detailed it becomes, the easier it is to trust.

Now we have complete faith in the process and know that we can take anybody, of any age or skill level, through it to make a surfboard. All we ask of them is that they bring a healthy amount of enthusiasm, patience, energy and optimism. I'm not saying that it's an easy thing to make, but by having a process that we have complete faith in, it becomes easier. Just one step following on from the last until we reach our goal of creating a beautiful finished item.

So, as you can see, if your process starts out as one of trial and error, over time you will be able to refine, adjust and strengthen your trust in, and the depth of, the process you develop. It keeps you on track.

Let's go back to something as simple as your morning cup of coffee. You start off knowing you need to grind the beans, mix them with hot (but not too hot) water and filter it. So you find a way to do this and then you taste the coffee. All you ever do from that point forward is experiment and adapt the hundreds of iterations until you find a process that works so that every time you make a coffee exactly how you like it. Then you trust that process.

A few years back, I was privileged to hear an incredible speech by Greg Long, a professional surfer who has made a career from surfing some of the world's largest waves. He wanted the audience to relate to what he did and used the phrase, 'One man's craziness is another man's reality'. Although this had a specific meaning for him, I find it interesting to draw the parallels to what I'm talking about here. The process we use in our five-day workshop may seem completely overwhelming. If I were to explain every single step, you'd think embarking on the journey would be crazy and yet that process is one I know like the back of my hand.

The magic for me comes when this craziness becomes a reality for the people who embark on the journey as they interact, play and engage with the process. The ability to trust in the process comes from testing it multiple times and knowing that the outcome is, more often than not, going to be the one desired. Therefore, the more it's put into action and tested, the more trusted it becomes, and the more it moves from feeling like craziness to a reality.

And finally, one of the most brilliant things about having a process you trust is that you can be more present in each and every moment, and simply enjoy the act of making. There is no need to worry about what was behind you, and there is no desire to consider the next steps. Sometimes, it can be helpful to understand the reasoning behind some of the targets or actions, but only to help calm and settle an inquisitive mind. All you need to do is focus on and immerse yourself in what is right in front of you, right here, right now. The present moment.

Trust the process.

Trust your senses

As part of immersing yourself in, and focusing on, the present moment, we need to learn to tune in to our senses too.

The sense of smell can be one of the most powerful elements to bring you into the present moment. When you step into someone's workshop, it is likely that one of the first things you notice is the smell — especially if, like me, they work with wood. I would encourage you to take that cue to pause and take a few deep breaths through your nose. Not only will it help calm your whole body and mind, it will start to trigger memories and emotions related to the smells. It may be a ceramicist's workshop where a smell of damp clay lingers in the air that reminds you of playing in the earth and mud as a child. Or a metal fabricator's workshop with a heavy, steely smell in the air. As you may have guessed, for me, nothing beats the smell of freshly cut timber. Each species has its own unique aroma and when you cut into it, it can stir a specific memory and take the level of absorption and enjoyment up a notch.

The sense of sound can be helpful when focusing on specific techniques. Once you tune in, you'll be able to hear how effective you are being with a saw or a plane. When the technique used is ineffective, you will hear a strange or unusual sound. Let that cue guide you into finding a path with less resistance. There will be a smooth rhythm to the sound as well as the action.

When making, we're naturally drawn to, and rely most heavily on, our sense of sight. The eyes are magical tools and they give you constant feedback on how you are shaping the world around you. They are literally making sense of the three-dimensional space we are in and allowing us to interpret that in our own way. However, they can be misleading, so we shouldn't rely on them too much. When you see a potter working at a wheel, you will likely notice that while they are watching what their hands are doing, they often can't see the actual piece of clay they are throwing. They are watching, but letting their eyes take a back seat to their sense of touch, which is often far more trustworthy when it comes to making.

I wonder if that is why we often instinctively reach out to touch things that we know have been made by hand. I think we all know that our eyes can only tell us part of the story and that our sense of touch helps gives us a more truthful account of what lies in front of us.

I find that when making things out of wood, the grain can cause confusion. The patterns within the grain can play tricks with your eyes and so it's often easier to look away while you run your hands over an object so you can focus more clearly on what it is telling you. The more making you do, the more you will learn to trust your sense of touch.

Nothing is as honest and seemingly complex to understand as the sense of touch. It seems as though nothing can lie to the hands, the fingers, the fingertips. They feel every lump and bump in shapes and are often our first port of call when we come into contact with a new object. We reach out and touch it to try to make sense of the shape it is occupying in space. This is especially evident when you make things out of timber. It is an almost uncontrollable reaction to seeing something shaped out of wood, to reach out and touch it, run your fingers along it and feel connected to it.

By focusing on the feedback coming through each of our senses, we can learn more and more about the processes we are involving ourselves in, and the deeper that practice goes, the more rewarding and all-encompassing the experience is.

6
**Slow making,
flow making**

That slow tempo of craftwork, of taking
the time you need to do something well,
is profoundly stabilising to individuals.

Richard Sennett

Driven by the industrial revolution, our Western culture
celebrates the instant. If the time taken to get from A to B
can be shortened, then the behaviour, tool or device
that enables that is rewarded. Our digital world has
exacerbated the systemic belief that faster is better,
and taken it to heights that seemed unfathomable only
a decade ago. Yet, as we are now witnessing, the fast-
paced world we live in is ultimately damaging — to the
planet and to ourselves. As more of us recognise this,
it feels like we are moving into a time of transition. One
driven by the very simple human need for connection.

As more people struggle with the fact that their waking
hours are spent working and interacting in an intangible
digital world, we need to find ways to reconnect. By that,
I mean reconnecting with the natural world; reconnecting
with the people around us, especially our loved ones; and
reconnecting to meaningful, tangible work. It is my belief
that all these things can be attained through the simple act
of making something.

On the fringes of our society, we have seen a movement
where slowing down is the aim. A growing number of people
are wanting to connect back to what it means to be human.

They have realised the power and the significance of slowing things down a bit: slow living, slow food, slow fashion and slow travel are all born from a reaction to the fast pace that permeates all aspects of our lives.

When we run our workshop courses, we do all we can to eliminate the use of machines. Originally, this was guided by a simple need. Letting unqualified and unskilled people loose on machinery was a risk and, unsurprisingly, prohibitively expensive to insure. So, we looked at our process and worked out how to navigate through it by hand. The machining typically happens in the preparation of the materials, so as long as we retained control of that part, the construction and shaping could be done relatively easily by hand. However, we soon realised there was actually a huge benefit to having to do so much of the making by hand.

Using *only* hand tools forces you to slow down.

Working with your hands

Remember the traditional bellyboard? The old wooden ones? There may be one lying in your parents' loft from family holidays spent on beaches. We run a one-day workshop to make one of these. During the day, only hand tools are used. Through a refined process that we teach, our customers are able to walk away with a physical reminder of what a day working with their hands can look like. On top of that, they have a new toy to go and play with in the ocean, creating family memories of their own.

Even though it's only a few hours of their time, we see people settle in quickly and get completely absorbed in the tasks. At the end of the day, we often hear them say how fast time has gone and that it was the best six hours of therapy they have ever had. For me, this is an ode to the benefits of slowing down, taking our time, becoming more considered in our actions, and working with care and sensitivity.

When we work with our hands, no element or process can be rushed. Hand tools can be incredibly unforgiving. If you try to go quickly, your technique will falter, you will inevitably make mistakes and the whole process requires more effort. This can often lead to cramping. The only way to achieve great results easily is to trust the process and slow down. There is no way to cheat. No life hacks here.

We see the real impact of slowing down on our longer, five-day, surfboard-making classes. We always limit numbers to a maximum of three people. It's true, three really is a magic number. There is something special about this group size that allows some deep connections to form. It is large enough to have a real chemistry, but small enough to feel incredibly safe. People feel inspired and excited, but also welcomed and comfortable.

With those five days, we have structured the workshops in a way that allows people to really settle into the space, leave their egos at the door, and come in and connect with us and each other on a really personal and human level. Then, through the process, we allow them to slow down. For some people, simply slowing down and reconnecting to craft and other people can be a profound reminder of what it is that makes them tick and can even inform some pretty huge life decisions. When this happens, it's magical to see and hear about.

Slowing down allows us to enjoy the journey. Recently, a customer said how much he was trying to make sure he enjoyed the process. As the week progresses, there are a number of fairly repetitive tasks. It can feel like the consequences of your actions are growing in significance and it's easy to get caught up in your own (analytical and often self-deprecating) thoughts of worry and anxiety. Checking in to the present moment and enjoying it was something he had to actively remind himself to do. It helped him to acknowledge that this was a once-in-a-lifetime experience, so it was important not to race to the end, but to enjoy the journey.

By the end of the week, he was amazed at how quickly it seemed to pass. For me, this can be an indicator of how well the course has gone for everyone. A question I often ask towards the end is, 'How long ago does Monday morning feel to you?' Surprisingly, while time seems to have flown past, it also feels like an awful lot has changed. For most people, Monday morning seems like a distant memory.

It's funny how time opens up when you slow things down a little.

Reconnecting with our hands, other people and the natural world can have a huge impact. It's no surprise that there is such a shift in our culture to be more 'present' and 'mindful'. Quite simply, people want to be more human again. We're human *beings*, not human to-do lists, after all.

The conflict

When I think about slowing down the process of making, it feels like a conflicting idea. More often than not we work to deadlines, either set by other people, or by ourselves. Quite often I feel the pressure of 'needing' to get a particular task finished by the end of the day. At times, it can be incredibly stressful.

Naturally, I have looked for ways to solve this problem and tried to identify where this stress is coming from. Why am I creating this sense of 'needing' to get things done? Why the urgency?

Typically, it comes from wanting to please the customer. Of course, this is an honourable thing to do and something we need to do as a business. But when you find yourself working for the fifth, sixth, seventh late night in a row, for the fifth, sixth, seventh week in a row, you realise that there must be something else at play here. This isn't a sustainable way either to live or run a business, so what is going on?

Early on, I was convinced it was passion, driven by a dream of business 'success'. Then I felt that it was all part of the artist's struggle. Of course I would have to work long hours. A life where I get to surf a couple of times each week, live a short walk from the beach and do what I truly enjoy every day can't come without its difficulties!

Gradually I've come to realise that when I choose to stay late to satisfy a self-imposed deadline, it is often me actively choosing to place a customer's need above my own. I need to recognise that the elevated feelings of stress keeping me there — increased heart rate, stiffened muscles and a shortness of breath — are signs of my body warning me that I'm not being true to myself.

In those moments of stress and anxiety, I am believing a story that is encouraged, supported and rewarded in the capitalist consumerism that permeates all of Western culture. I am believing the story that this product will make my customer happy, that a person's happiness is controlled by elements outside of themself, by material possessions. I am believing a story that I know not to be true. And my body reacts.

When I recognise those signs of stress, it's a signal to stop and reflect. While my judgement and awareness can sometimes be off, I find that when I *don't* stay late, the job or task that was holding me in the workshop simply rolls on to the next day's to-do list or even falls off the list altogether.

Actively slowing things down, taking time and enjoying the processes involved in each stage of making all help to create a better end product. You will find that each item you make will get better, one at a time, and life will feel more balanced and healthy as a result.

Slowing the making down gives you a chance to breathe, to relax, and the more you can focus your senses on each and every movement, the more purposeful and considered each one becomes. It allows for easier physical and mental absorption. By working almost exclusively with your hands and hand tools, you will find a deeper and stronger connection to the object you are making.

There is a beauty in the simplicity of it.

Finding flow

Over the last few years, understanding of and research into the 'flow state' has deepened considerably. It seems to be the golden key to unlocking the potential of any human on the planet, regardless of their pursuit. In a nutshell, there is a cycle of four experiences that flow is a part of: struggle, release, flow and recovery.

Moments of insight, wisdom and peace often come during periods of meditative or 'flow' states, and completely absorbing yourself in the making process can help you get there. First you need to really challenge yourself, push yourself to the limit of your comfort zone. Then you need to find a way to release yourself and simply focus on being in the moment, with all of your senses. Through practice, the hope is that you experience a state of flow, where a sense of space and time can seem to warp and even your sense of self becomes distorted. Finally, there is the state of recovery, where you need to come down from this heightened experience and prepare to embark on it all over again.

By pushing yourself to delve deeper into small, individual processes and allowing yourself, mind and body, to become absorbed in them, you'll find that you begin to look at the object you're working on in more and more detail. Your focus heightens.

Originally, when I began to try to wrap my head around my passion for things that involved total absorption, I noticed a similarity in the state of mind that they provoked: a total surrender to the present moment. I'd understood this to be searching for a sense of escapism, because in those moments, there is no space left in your brain for other thoughts. But I was confused: what was I trying to escape from?

Over time I came to realise, it wasn't escape. I wasn't running from anyone or anything, I was actively seeking out pursuits and opportunities that got me into a flow state. Today, these fleeting moments are one of the primary motivators for me to continue to make surfboards and to surf.

While the making of one surfboard — or anything, for that matter — can never last forever, exploring the process of making can. For me, one surfboard simply leads on to the next. But we still have to learn how to recognise the feeling of something being finished, which is often one of the most challenging moments to recognise. If you are making in order to explore processes to learn from, this can be a relatively light decision, but if you are searching for an idea of something you have seen in your mind's eye, the finish line can seem like it is never going to appear. It is always, tantalisingly, just over the horizon.

It's as hard to get from
almost finished to finished
as to get from beginning
to almost done.

Elinor Fuchs

When it comes to making, the decision of where to stop is something you will confront; or, in some ways, it will confront you. As the maker responsible for bringing this new creation into the world, when you decide it's finished, you feel it's out there for the world to judge. Not only that, but it is what you consider to be your best effort, your idea of perfect. You feel an attachment to the object as though it somehow reflects who you are, or at least your own standards. Interestingly though, everyone who judges the object will never know it with the intimacy that you do.

Perfectionism is a personal standard, attitude or philosophy that demands 'perfect' and rejects anything less. In recent years, its pursuit has been shown to correlate with the amount of stress that an individual suffers from. That's a difficult pill to swallow when you stop to consider how this character trait has been revered by parents, teachers, peers and bosses throughout our lives. We live in a society that rewards 'perfect' achievements and uses them as a way of judging success. It's no wonder so many of us like to consider ourselves a 'perfectionist', and it can be easy to overlook how this can often lead to depression and severe anxiety. Perfectionism is shrouded in shame and judgement.

If we hold perfectionism so close to our heart, we no longer see failures as opportunities to learn. Any failure becomes a weighty burden to carry — and a reason for self-punishment.

> It's always helpful to remember that when perfectionism is driving, shame is riding shotgun.
> Perfectionism is not healthy striving.
> It is not asking, 'How can I be my best self?'
> Instead, it's asking, 'What will people think?'
>
> Brené Brown

Central to the idea of perfectionism is that perfect objects, places and even people actually exist. Yet if we all have our unique experience of the world we live in, surely the only way that perfection would exist is if we all, unanimously, agreed on something being perfect. Each and every individual in the world would have to agree that the object you are making is perfect. Now, does that seem like a realistic, fair and healthy goal?

Early on, I was obsessed with the outcome of my making and my own idea of perfection. Being a 'perfectionist' was something I was proud of. However, as the years have passed, my idea of perfectionism and craftsmanship has evolved. I used to find it difficult to separate the two, and thought that one simply led to the other. Now I find it helpful to remember that nothing in this world is permanent, so your 'finished' object is always going to be in a state of flux.

It's far better to inhabit a place of learning: trusting the process and enjoying the journey.

Craftsmanship

As practice makes perfect, I cannot but make progress; each drawing one makes, each study one paints, is a step forward.

Vincent van Gogh

The idea of craftsmanship is a constant striving for excellence, not perfection. With an awareness that perfection is not real, not even attainable, we begin to understand that we are simply on a journey and each time we attempt something we are taking a step further forward. Being conscious about the reality of your outcome is a far healthier place to operate from. We can occupy a space of optimism and hope, not fear and regret.

Those who reach the top of their game, who are considered to be the best in the world at what they do, are rarely driven by a desire for perfection. This doesn't mean to say that a pursuit of perfection can't lead to greatness, but it can be limiting in its nature. It is a restrictive and judgemental way of looking at the world, rather than being open, honest and authentic.

If you have seen the film *Free Solo* about the free climber Alex Honnold then you'll recognise this example (if you haven't seen it, you must, because it is an incredible story of one of the sporting world's greatest individual achievements as Alex free solo climbs Yosemite's El Capitan without ropes or safety gear).

In the film, there is a section when Alex sits alongside his mother and they talk about how, when he was growing up, a piece of her advice stuck with him: 'Good enough, isn't.' When watching it, you can understand how this way of thinking could have pushed him to achieve such incredible performances in the climbing world and, ultimately, to be considered as one of the best climbers who ever lived. However, it also seems to be a heavy burden rather than a piece of advice. Clearly, Alex managed to use this idea of constantly bettering himself to rise to an incredible level of skill. He has been able to use it to fuel his striving for excellence, but I'm not sure it would have had the same effect on everyone. If you can frame your making as striving for excellence rather than perfectionism, it will be far healthier and more enjoyable.

The art of finishing

From my own experience, if you become obsessed with the idea that the object you're making needs to be perfect, it poses some real problems.

For one thing, it becomes incredibly hard to decide the point at which you consider the object to be 'finished'. I often say a surfboard is finished knowing full well that I could spend another few hours or even days refining it. It is possibly the scariest part of the process for me as I have to let go of the learned behaviour of being a perfectionist.

Almost all surfboards are made with the intention of being symmetrical. That is to say, having the same outline, rail shape, thickness and width on the left-hand side as there is on the right. That way they should perform the same way when surfing either right or left on a wave. The symmetry provides balance in the way the board feels underfoot. So, when you are working on one side of the board, you then need to replicate it on the other side. This is tricky, especially when you consider that you are right- or left-handed, so the techniques you use on one side will need to be adapted to create the same result on the other.

Despite my own perfectionist tendencies and struggle with declaring an object finished, I was having a conversation with another maker about this very issue and he seemed to have little or no trouble calling his own work 'finished'. He said that the reason he never worried about it was that by saying one was finished, he was giving himself the opportunity to start the next one. The end was just the beginning of the next one, and if you took forward all your learnings, you were likely to make something better next time. In which case, why not call something finished as soon as you can and get started on a new one?

Shifting perspectives

When making, the idea of a constant process, with no true beginning or end point, is a fresh perspective. Personally, I've found that the times when I struggle are when we're working on a custom piece with a clearly defined start *and* end point!

For example, we recently made a surfboard for the charity Surfers Against Sewage. It was going to be presented to HRH The Prince of Wales. He was to sign the board as a celebration of the charity's 30-year anniversary and to signify becoming its patron. We had managed to speak with his estate management team at Highgrove House to see if there was any timber they had that we could incorporate into the board. They were happy to help and offered us a couple of oak planks and a round of wood from HRH's favourite tree — the iconic 200-year-old cedar of Lebanon that used to stand in the centre of his garden. Sadly, the tree was suffering from a fungal disease and had to be taken down in 2008.

So, we had a tight deadline, a very limited source of unique timber, and the final board was going to be seen and signed by the Prince of Wales himself. In addition, all of the press and invited guests would have a chance to get up close to it too.

Of course, I wanted this board to be perfect. I had to actively remind myself that my best is more than good enough, and not to worry about how others might judge me and my work. In the end, I got the board finished, but it was without a fin. I had hoped to have one fitted in time for the event — even though our fins are always fitted after the finishing resin is applied, which would need to come *after* the grand signing. Still, I was worried about how press images of a surfboard without a fin would reflect on our company, or that people would think it was half-finished. I had to take a breath, stand back and admire what lay in front of me: a surfboard that encapsulated and reflected 10 years of refining a craft. A surfboard that in its own right was stunning and beautiful, even enhanced by some of its imperfections. I had to stop myself from getting overwhelmed and obsessed by the small details that *I* could see were not 'perfect'.

Knowing when to stop is a crucial skill for a maker and, just like all of the other skills, it is one that we will all continue to learn about — and probably struggle with. All I can say is that I find that the point at which you consider something finished is more of a feeling than anything else. Only you can decide when what you are making is truly finished. And it is good to remember that by acknowledging this feeling, we are both releasing and allowing ourselves to start making something else. Something exciting and new.

POWER

8
Belief

There is no such word as *can't*.

My primary school teacher

Having this idea instilled in me when I was very young has definitely made it stick. Now, whenever I find myself thinking or saying I can't do something, a little alarm goes off in my head to say, 'Hold on, you *can* do it, but you've got to fully understand how much you want it.' Maybe it would be more helpful to borrow the phrase from David Allen: 'You can do anything, but not everything.'

You get to choose the things that you want to invest time and energy in until you can do them, and the things that you don't. Every now and then, someone comes into the workshop believing the story that they *can't* make a surfboard. Their starting mindset, despite having signed up to a week-long course, is certainty that they will be the first person to 'fail' the week and walk away without a surfboard. They genuinely believe they 'can't' do things — and that they definitely can't do this.

For me, this way of thinking is quite alien because I've always believed that it's more a question of how much you want it. However when a good friend opened up about this being his 'go-to' emotional state when confronted with new things, it became apparent that this feeling of 'not being able to do something' may be more common that I first thought and often comes with a large amount of baggage and history.

It seems to link back to a fundamental belief of not being 'good enough'. Often people who have been successful at many things in life, from their careers to their personal relationships, can have a deep-seated feeling of imposter syndrome. They don't feel worthy of their own accomplishments and believe they're a fraud living a lie. Self-doubt takes root and permeates their lives.

So, how do we change this mindset so we're not put off making before we've even started? After all, we're all born makers, right?

For me, interactions with these types of makers are often the most rewarding. You see their self-awareness open up and they become more willing to simply 'have a go'. This is crucial in our workshops, because for them to feel a sense of ownership of their board, they need to have a large part in the making process. It wouldn't be the same if they simply watched us make a board over five days then hand it over. And this is where trusting the process is really key. One step at a time, we help them work their way forward.

Usually, over the first couple of days they begin to relax into the space. They gain more confidence using the tools and, more importantly, in their own hands. I see this happen as they look to me less for guidance. They start to reach for the glues and the clamps on their own, and to cognitively understand the way all the pieces of wood fit together in order to reach the desired outcome.

As we move into the shaping phase, the use of tools for shaping and sanding the wood becomes more and more critical as we get closer to the finished form. The pressure of the week begins to build and I find it important for me to start stepping back from the process as people work their way through the ever-finer sanding blocks. By this point, they have become much more in tune with the tools, understanding how best to apply each one to manipulate the form of the wood as needed. They develop an understanding of the feedback loop involving their hands, trusting in their sense of touch that felt alien to them only a few days before, and finally, they will even decide for themselves the moment of completion.

This is where the most magical part of the process is for the people who joined us with little self-confidence and the strong belief that they would fail.

In front of them is a surfboard. It is an undeniable physical representation of their own abilities and it often far exceeds even their greatest expectations.

If we could capture and sell the way people feel on the Friday afternoon, we would be millionaires. But alas, the feelings are all felt deep within the individuals and wouldn't fit in any bottle I know of.

Dan was one such customer. He came a few years ago to make a board, and I now consider him to be an incredibly close friend. His surfboard now hangs on the wall of his office. It has become the perfect reminder that he is a person who *can* do things. And whenever he doubts his abilities as an author, CEO, friend, husband, father, he can look up at the surfboard and remind himself of his abilities to do anything he puts his mind — and hands — to.

I've never increased my confidence so much in one week — and I never knew that making a surfboard could do that!

Dan Kieran

He had developed a narrative for himself which defined what he could and couldn't do, and he had stuck to it. That was right up until he came and made a surfboard with us. Suddenly, he had proved that the narrative was meaningless. By making something — by himself — that he had never thought possible, he was able to reset his understanding of what *was* possible. The experience was so impactful for him that he even ended up writing a book about it, *The Surfboard*.

9
**A shared
experience**

Holding on to anything is like
holding on to your breath.
You will suffocate.

Deepak Chopra

**I find making surfboards an incredibly powerful process
to immerse myself in because of how it grounds me
and connects me back to nature — through the wood,
the ocean and my own hands. It gives me the space and
time to calm my mind and find a quietness that is often
missing in day-to-day life. But the biggest impact it has
had on me is the way it has allowed me to connect with
other people — which is surprising, given making is
largely regarded as a solitary activity.**

Sharing the experience of making was not something I
had ever planned to do. The first time it happened was
all down to an enquiry. After spending two or three years
refining the boards I was making, I started to put them out
into the world. Two boards were on display at a local craft
gallery and one chap, Steve, saw them and immediately
reached out to me.

He lived a couple of villages further up the coast and
was a keen surfer. He wanted to come to the workshop
to see the boards and talk about them. After a long
conversation with him over several cups of tea, I thought
this was going to be one of my first sales. But he changed
the course of the conversation. He said that as much as

he loved the boards, he was also really passionate about making things out of wood and he wondered if I would be able to help him through the process of making one of his own. In all honesty, I felt threatened by what he was asking. I was only just starting to sell some of the surfboards after spending months and months refining the process — and here was someone who wanted me to pass on all of that knowledge in a matter of days? I felt really vulnerable having invited him into the workshop. Had I already said too much?

When you position yourself in the niche of an already tiny industry, competition can feel very threatening, especially at such an early stage.

Was I prepared to share everything I had worked through with a stranger in the hope that it would be a beneficial experience for us both? Or should I keep my cards close to my chest at this crucial, early-growth stage of a new business?

I needed time to consider it and went home to speak to my partner, now wife, Liz. We discussed the potential outcomes from both scenarios and found that, ultimately, sharing the knowledge felt like a more wholesome route to take. It might look scary, but if Steve wanted to go through the process of making his own board, maybe there would be others. Sharing the experience with Steve could be a way for me to see if the process would suit a course format.

Steve agreed to be my guinea pig and we broke his sessions down to one afternoon per week over 12 weeks. As it turned out, that surfboard I made with Steve was to be the second surfboard to change my life. By sharing the knowledge I had accumulated, I was able to take Steve on the journey I had experienced while making my first surfboard back in my student days. Over the course of the sessions, he grew in confidence in and around the workshop and there were points where I could easily let him get on with it on his own. As we got towards the end of the making, he became obsessed with thinking about how the board would feel in the water. How would it paddle? How would it feel to catch that first wave? How would the board feel under his feet? He began to experience the emotions I had, a real excitement and anticipation for the future of the board.

This, for me, is where making a wooden surfboard is unique. It is a piece of equipment that you will be taking into a dynamic and thrilling environment, using it to interact with the energy moving through the ocean. As a wave approaches, you draw on all of your experience to try to predict how it's going to break so you can surf it and enjoy the ride. You become excited by what is about to happen, but you are simultaneously pulled into the present moment because of the demand on all your senses to respond to how the wave uniquely unfolds in front of you. You don't plan these magical moments, you only experience them as they happen. Making a surfboard to experience these moments with is truly special, and it's why I struggle to put that feeling into words.

One thing you learn from surfing is how to operate in the present. It's really what the whole surfing experience is about.

—

Gerry Lopez

Being able to share these feelings and emotions with people has become the part of my time as a maker that I hold closest to my heart. It is truly wonderful to be able to share these experiences with others — they create such a strong connection between us. Making together not only reconnects people to working with their own two hands and the materials they use, it also reconnects people with people, creating a space for meaningful understanding and empathy towards one another.

Each time we run a workshop course, we don't know who is going to walk through the door on the Monday morning. Obviously, we'll have had some contact with them, but we don't really know them as people.

Every person brings with them their own story, their own journey and their own values and points of view, as well as their own reason for joining us. This gives every workshop its own character and it is this variety in the experience that I truly love about sharing the act of making with others.

The most magical workshops have to be when the week is shared with family and loved ones. Most years, we'll have one or two family groups who come and join us. Husbands and wives, parents and children or siblings. When people bring such a deep personal connection into the workshop, it's really amazing to see how the week unfolds for them. A couple of years ago a father and son joined us. While they were clearly already close, the time spent together was unusual — neither had their own agenda, or needs that had to be met. There was no jostling of schedules. All they needed to do was turn up each day and be present with me and with each other. Over the week, I could see how close their bond was and I felt privileged to be a part of it.

A few months later, I reached out to see how they were getting on and the conversation soon came back to the week spent in the workshop.

The father, Justin, told me that there had been two main benefits to the week spent together. Firstly, they both had beautiful surfboards that they had made themselves and that gave them an excuse to plan surfing trips together. Secondly — and the reflection that brought a tear to my eye — was how he admitted that in the busyness of day-to-day life it was easy to simply co-exist and not really *see* each other, but by spending the week together, he saw for the first time what a beautiful young man his son was growing up to be.

Having such an effect on people, forging relationships between complete strangers and, most uniquely, strengthening relationships between family members, makes me feel unbelievably privileged and lucky. The hairs go up on the back of my neck just thinking about it! Making things together can do that.

The act of making can have an incredible impact on us as individuals, but the real power found through working with your hands comes when it is also felt through your heart.

10
**Making
ourselves**

When you get rid of your fear of failure, your tensions about succeeding ...
you can be yourself. Relaxed. You'll no longer be driving with your brakes on.

Anthony de Mello

I feel so lucky to have found something that I was passionate about at such a young age. I was able, with love and support from those around me, to follow that passion and carry it with me. The path that has led me here has been guided by my love for people and the environment, so I would implore you to do the same. Follow your heart and stick to what you enjoy, because you'll end up living a life you love.

For various reasons, but mostly because I was challenged recently by a close friend, I started to question where this passion and direction came from. The friend encouraged me to dig deep and I found that underneath everything that we experience, if we strip it all away, we are left with love. At our core, we all have love and compassion for the planet, love for each other and love for ourselves. Making something can be a great reminder of this.

During the course of writing this book, it became impossible to ignore the parallels between the process of making a physical object with our own two hands, and that of making ourselves.

You could say that we all enter this world as a blank canvas, an empty vessel. We go through the various stages of shaping and building on the path of progress. Over time we strip away the excess that doesn't serve us. We are constantly improving, learning and overcoming challenges as we go through more stages of reshaping and rebuilding, being drawn along a path that is guided by who we feel we are.

There are times that we feel broken or bruised but, like the wood in my hands, I know that those parts can be reworked and strengthened, or appreciated as one part of our story. They add to the character and to the narrative.

At times, we can feel overworked and underappreciated, deflated and downtrodden. We need to recognise that in those moments, more than ever, we need to nurture ourselves — to sand out those knocks and scrapes, and apply another layer of protective oil.

The result of all our work will never be finished. We're not born finished and we certainly don't die finished. But the journey between the two points will be beautiful and of real value to this world. That's where the magic will be.

The physical object in which I see these parallels so clearly is that of the handplane. And I'd encourage you to have a go at making one by following the how-to guide at the back of the book. When I think about making a handplane, it's easy to get caught up in the seriousness of the process, the decisions and the practicality of it. Yet when all is said and done, the ultimate purpose is to use it to immerse yourself in the elements, feel the energy of the ocean, connect back to nature, to yourself, and enjoy the ride.

Play.

Laugh.

Share.

Epilogue

It has nothing to do with surfboards.

It has very little to do with what you are making.

Making is simply a process that facilitates and promotes a headspace for reflection, as well as an openness to connect —to the physical world, yes, but also to the people and places around us. Through making we become more in tune with what makes us human, and that is compassion, love and connection.

Maybe that's the most magical thing about making something, making anything. It gives you the space to form connections. By creating an environment for people to make, and guiding them through the process, we enable them to do this, as well as giving them physical skills that last a lifetime.

Life coach Tony Robbins isn't for everyone, but he has spoken extensively about the six human needs, which is something I have found useful when it comes to understanding individual motives or thought processes behind behaviour. They are:

- **Certainty**
- **Uncertainty / Variety**
- **Significance**
- **Love / Connection**
- **Growth**
- **Contribution**

Tony Robbins has worked with thousands of individuals over his lifetime. He believes that each and every one of us has these needs, but we prioritise them in our own way. If we can satisfy three of our needs at the same time, we experience something meaningful, and if we can satisfy four or more of them, we will often experience something that we desperately seek and this could become addictive.

So, let's apply this to making. If we consider the needs that are met by making something, we tick the certainty box straight away. We are certain that we are going to make a physical change to the material or object in front of us.

The uncertainty comes the minute we start making, because while we are hoping to achieve a certain outcome, each mark we make, each cut of the saw or strike of the chisel, can bring about a different result. There is an excitement and nervousness that comes from the uncertainty.

Our sense of significance can increase through making, because of the way it gives us a purpose, a goal or a target. The idea being that, in some way, you make the world a better place through what you are making.

Connection is an easy one. Not only do we become much more connected to our own senses and the object we are making, we also feel more connected to the materials we are using. Ultimately, the minute you present your object to the world, it becomes a talking point and something that connects you to other people.

By this point making something has already ticked four of the human needs. So based on Tony's observations, the process is likely to be fairly memorable depending on how individuals prioritise these needs.

Growth is something that will develop as you learn new skills. With them, a sense of confidence and self-belief will come.

Contribution can be the trickier need to satisfy through making. Often when we start making, it is something that we do for ourselves. But the more you make, the more you will want to share the objects you make and the skills you learn. As the time you spend making develops, you will most likely start to feel a deeper sense of contribution.

That's certainly what I have come to find through sharing the experience of making, rather than being one man in a shed making things. For me, involving other people in the process and making something that I am passionate about are the most fulfilling things I have ever done.

By making something, you have the opportunity to experience and interact with your basic human needs. I hope that you can use the process to connect back to yourself, understand what really makes you tick, and apply those lessons to the rest of your life.

Our hands are the main physical connection we have to the world around us. They represent how we connect to the world and our surroundings. The journey of making that we take people on ends up having very little to do with the actual surfboard, but the fact that it is a surfboard contributes an extra level of excitement and passion, which I think compounds the power of those five days.

The power that was always there all along.

The power within your own two hands.

Good luck on your making adventures! Enjoy them.

I'd love to see what you make. Feel free to share images and use the hashtag *#DoMake*.

Appendix

How to make a handplane
A step-by-step guide

What you will need

— 1 × handplane blank (see page 106)
— 1 × pencil
— 1 × straight edge or ruler
— 1 × sheet of paper or card for making a template
— 1 × wood saw
— 1 × rasp (a file to shape wood)
— 2 × clamps
— 1 × sanding block
— Several grades of sandpaper
— 1 × bottle of tung oil (or similar) and a lint-free rag
  for application

Clearing a space

It's a good idea to clear a space on a workbench or table. You will be generating sawdust and sanding dust, so make sure you're able to clear up easily. Or, if weather permits and you have access to some outdoor space, you might find it enjoyable to work outside.

I always find it easiest to work from the corner of a table or workbench so part of the handplane hangs off for easier cutting and rasping (and hopefully minimising the risk of damage to your table). So, ensure you have good access to a nice clear corner section.

We will be doing most of the work with the top side of the handplane facing down and the underside (with the pencil-drawn templates) facing up. To hold the handplane in place while you are using the saw or rasp, it is best to use a couple of clamps.

Make sure the surface you are working on is smooth and clear of any dust or lumps, as the wood can mark easily. It's worth keeping surfaces clear throughout the making process.

Towards the end, when you get into the sanding, you may find it helpful to lay a cloth on the table to reduce the risk of picking up any marks or dents.

Finally, before we begin, it's worth reminding yourself that you can always take more wood off, but you can't add it back on! So take it steady, enjoy the process and know that there is no 'right' or 'wrong' way to do it.

Your handplane blank

You're going to need a piece of wood slightly bigger than your open hand. On our courses, we give you a pre-prepared 'blank', measuring 45cm long × 22cm wide × 1.5cm thick.

You could purchase some timber from a local supplier, or repurpose some wood that you already have at home. Alternatively, you can buy one of our kits which come with a 'blank' to get you started (just go to the Product page on our website: *ottersurfboards.co.uk*). In terms of the type of wood, we tend to use cedar and poplar simply because those are the timbers we use for our surfboard construction. They are lightweight and are grown and harvested sustainably and locally. However, any wood will do! Bear in mind that the heavier it is, the more cumbersome it feels in the water. For simplicity, a piece of plywood would work fine.

Picking your shape

Once you have your blank in front of you, you need to decide on a template, or shape, for your handplane.

Typically, the larger the handplane, the more lift and speed you will be able to generate in the water, but the less manoeuvrable it will be. We find that something about 5–7cm wider than your hand and 10–15cm longer than your whole, open hand is a really good place to start.

You can create your own template using paper or card (you can base it on the image on page 104). You will find it easier to only draw half of it, with a straight line on the other side, so that when you have cut out your template and come to draw it onto your piece of wood, you can simply put the straight line in the centre and flip it over to mirror the shape on each side.

The outlines of our templates take their inspiration from classic surfboards, but we have also experimented with some shapes that seem to match the dimensions of our hands better. Relating the shapes back to our hands and making them more human in their design seems to be the best way to go. In all honesty, while there are differences in how the

Top
Picking your shape and
marking out your template

Bottom
Removing the excess
timber slowly and gently

shapes feel in the water, we encourage people to pick a shape that they are most drawn to or simply like the look of.

Using a pencil, draw your chosen template on the *underside* of the piece of wood. Then if you get any tear out of the wood as you cut and shape it, it is more likely to be on the top of the handplane, which is less critical for its performance.

Removing the excess timber

Once you are set on the shape you would like to achieve, the next step is to remove the excess wood.

In the workshop we have a rack of Japanese pull-saws for doing this because we love their elegant design and, when you're working with one, it feels like the most natural and intuitive saw you've ever used. But any wood saw will do. I would encourage you to use a hand saw, rather than any electric tools. When using a hand saw, the two most important things to remember are *slowly* and *gently*. There is no prize for finishing quickly, and the only way you can improve your technique will be by sawing slowly enough that you can be aware of all of your movements. A saw will do the work for you, so you don't need to put any extra force or pressure into the cutting action. What we find is that when people do, they often tense up, and that's what causes cramping in the hand, wrist and forearm. Not to mention the errors that are more likely to occur.

At this stage, we're aiming to remove a large part of the excess timber, cutting to about 4mm outside of the line of our template. This leaves enough tolerance to allow for most inaccuracies, but also doesn't leave us with a mountain to climb in the next stage.

Cut a series of straight lines that come close to the outline of your template; don't try to bend the blade to follow any curves. Do your best to keep the saw blade perpendicular to the handplane blank too. This is to avoid undercutting the outline at any point.

Refining the template

Once you've removed all you can with the saw, swap down to a rasp, which is more like a file (see top image) and allows you to start shaping the blank.

You are aiming to keep the outline of the handplane perpendicular (square) to the bottom surface of the handplane at this point, so that the template stays true throughout the thickness of the handplane (see bottom image). You are aiming to remove all of the wood outside the pencil line of your template, but should still be able to see the pencil line at the end.

During this process, you will start to feel the outline of the handplane with your hands. You want to address any lumps and bumps in the shape to make it nice and smooth. The key here is to repeatedly use your fingers and thumbs to feel your way around the outline. They will spot lumps that your eyes cannot see.

Shaping the rails

Once the handplane shape follows the outline smoothly, start to look at and think about how it is going to interact with the water. This is when you'll shape the rails according to what will perform best. When we talk about the 'shape' of a rail, we are thinking about its cross-section (see top image on page 112).

A hard rail is one with a square edge on the bottom of it. It generates the most lift in the water so will work best. With this in mind, continue to use the rasp to round over

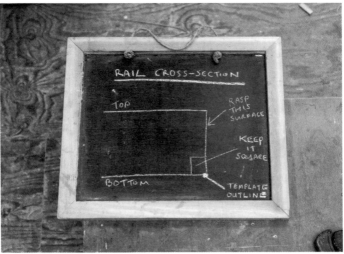

Top
Refining the template using
a Japanese saw rasp

Bottom
Keep the outline of the handplane
perpendicular to the bottom

Top
Shaping the rails to preserve
the hard edge on the bottom

Bottom
Use the rasp to round over
the top of the rail

the top of the rail. Make sure you don't touch the bottom 5mm so you can preserve that nice hard edge.

The amount you round over the top of the rail is up to you. It has little impact on the performance of the handplane; it's more a case of finding something that feels right to you.

Hand hole or strap?

When using your finished handplane, you have the option of gripping it via a hand hole or a hand strap. The hole is the simplest option to create at home.

The easiest way to make a hand hole would be to chain-drill (i.e. drill several holes close together) some large holes (25mm in diameter) where you want your fingers to protrude through the handplane and then rasp and sand the opening into a smooth shape. We use a template and a router to get the same hand hole in each of our handplanes (see top image on page 114).

In order to work out the best place for the hole to go, simply rest your open hand on the top of the handplane, in the centre. It should be just under the first knuckle join from your palm to your fingers.

Alternatively, if you like the idea of a strap, which will allow you to use the handplane with an open palm, this can be made out of any material and pinned to the handplane either side of your hand with screws and washers. Just make sure the screws don't go all the way through your handplane. We use some stainless-steel webbing bridges and custom-made straps out of repurposed seat belts and neoprene offcuts (see bottom image on page 114).

Top
A hand hole is the simplest
option to create at home

Bottom
A strap allows you to use the
handplane with an open palm

Sanding

Once you feel like you're getting close to your finished shape, you can start using the sandpaper and the sanding block.

If you only use your hand to support the sandpaper, you may well introduce ridges that follow the grain. By placing the sandpaper over a sanding block, you'll find it easier to achieve a smooth surface.

Use rougher (80 or 120 grit) sandpaper first and work your way over the whole handplane. Make sure that all of your movements follow the direction of the grain; you don't want to introduce any marks that go across the grain at this point as they become very hard to remove.

Once you've removed all the marks left by the rasp and run the sandpaper up and down the top and bottom surfaces, jump onto the next grade of sandpaper (180 grit) and do it all over again.

This is the process of refining your handplane. At this stage, rather than drastically changing the shape, you are taking away unnecessary marks until you reach the point where you feel like the handplane is finished.

Oiling and aftercare

Once you have finished all of the sanding and shaping, sign your handplane (we find a Biro works best) and begin oiling it. This is to preserve the wood and protect it from the elements. We use a natural tung oil to do this which comes from the tung nut. (NB in case you end up using your handplane as a chopping board, it is food safe). As the oil is chemical free, the curing time is quite slow: a minimum of 48 hours between coats.

You'll need two coats to be applied before first taking it into the water. Ideally, you'll build up to five to eight coats to get a really tough finish (the oil hardens over the coming days, weeks and months so your handplane will only get stronger over time). This extended curing time might not seem ideal but it means the environmental impact of the handplane is reduced. An alternative oil with a faster curing time is linseed oil.

Once the oil has cured, it's time to get out there. You need to get the handplane in the sea and test it in various conditions to learn how it behaves and how to use it to make the most of the waves!

Riding those waves was the objective when you started on this journey, so it's important that you try and get to a beach and take the time to enjoy this moment.

Crucial to the lifetime of your handplane will be how well you look after it. By continuing to oil your handplane, taking the time to sand out any nicks and dings and re-oiling it every few months if used regularly, you will ensure it lasts as long as possible. You may find that, after time, as you take it into the ocean more, it will inevitably pick up some damage. So be aware of this. Know that it will happen and learn how to look after it when it does. It is through the process of using it and creating memorable moments in the ocean, that you will become more connected and, hopefully, cherish it even more.

Resources

I find inspiration comes from so many individuals via an intricate network of connected experiences, all of which have helped shape this book. Some people you are fortunate enough to meet, others you may even work alongside and share time with. Some you listen to on podcasts and interviews, whilst others you watch on film and read about in books.

If you want to dig a little deeper into the world of making, the following resources will offer inspiration and a good place to start.

Books

Awareness
— Anthony De Mello

Cradle to Cradle: Remaking the Way We Make Things
— Michael Braungart and William McDonough

The Craftsman
— Richard Sennett

Endure: Mind, Body and the Curiously Elastic Limits of Human Performance
— Alex Hutchinson

The Green Imperative: Ecology and Ethics in Design and Architecture
— Victor Papanek

*Let My People Go Surfing:
The Education of a
Reluctant Businessman*
— Yvon Chouinard

*Lost Connections:
Uncovering the Real Causes
of Depression — and the
Unexpected Solutions*
— Johann Hari

*The Man Who Made Things
Out of Trees*
— Robert Penn

*The Power of Moments:
Why Certain Experiences
Have Extraordinary Impact*
— Chip Heath & Dan Heath

*The Rise: Creativity, the
Gift of Failure and the
Search for Mastery*
— Sarah Lewis

*The Rise of Superman:
Decoding the Science of
Ultimate Human Performance*
— Steven Kotler

Rising Strong
— Brené Brown

*The Surfboard: How Using
My Hands Helped Unlock
My Mind*
— Dan Kieran

*Trust the Process: An Artist's
Guide to Letting Go*
— Shaun McNiff

*What Has Nature Ever
Done for Us? How Money
Really Does Grow on Trees*
— Tony Juniper

The Wild Places
— Robert Macfarlane

*Wildwood: A Journey
Through Trees*
— Roger Deakin

*Zen and the Art of
Motorcycle Maintenance*
— Robert M. Pirsig

Magazines / Journals

The Surfer's Path
The Surfer's Journal

Talks

Do Schools Kill Creativity?
— Sir Ken Robinson

*The Mind is for Having Ideas,
Not Holding Them*
— David Allen

*You Think You Have Ideas,
But Ideas Have You*
— Dan Kieran

Podcasts

Finding Mastery
— Michael Gervais

How I Built This
— Guy Raz

Looking Sideways
— Matt Barr

The Peter Attia Drive

The Rich Roll Podcast

TED Radio Hour

The Tim Ferriss Show

The Tony Robbins Podcast

Under the Skin
— Russell Brand

YouTube

One platform that serves
makers so well is YouTube.
Here you can find guidance
on how to make almost
anything.

Other Makers

Tom Blake
Jake Boex
Matthew Burt
Ben Cook
Polly Macpherson
John Makepeace
Matthias
Tom Raffield
Roy Tam
Andrew Trotman
Kerry Whittle

About the Author

James is the founder of Otter Surfboards, where he designs and makes award-winning wooden surfboards that have been featured on television through *Countryfile* (BBC), *Escape to the Country* (BBC), *Made in Britain* (ITV) and *How It's Made* (Discovery Channel), and in print in *The Guardian*, *The Telegraph* and *GQ*.

As well as making wooden surfboards, he has led workshop courses for the past eight years, sharing his passion for making with others.

James has taken to the stage to inspire others to follow their hearts, reconnect to their hands and deepen their connection to the natural world at events such as Tedx Brighton and the Global Wave Conference.

He lives with his young family in Cornwall on a rugged stretch of coastline where the Atlantic meets the southern tip of the UK.

You can find out more at *jamesotter.co.uk*

For surfboards and workshop schedules, please visit *ottersurfboards.co.uk*

Thanks

Firstly, thank *you* for reading this book.

There are so many wonderful people and experiences that have shaped my story and my gratitude is for every single one of you. Friends, family, teachers, educators, makers, creatives, leaders, collaborators, photographers, writers and filmmakers.

In the creation of this book, my thanks go out to all of those who have helped bring it to life. It started at the Do Lectures in 2015 when I hosted a handplane-making workshop and met Miranda of the Do Book Co. Everything about the Do Lectures is inspiring, uplifting and beautiful, so thank you for allowing me to be a part of the story.

Thank you, Miranda, for helping to guide me through the writing process, something that at the outset was daunting and unfamiliar, but with your help became thoroughly enjoyable.

For the past eight years, I've been lucky enough to work with Mat Arney whose photography brings this book to colour, and to life. Thank you for your incredible support throughout and your beautiful imagery.

Thank you to those who I work alongside in the world of surfboard making and ocean activism, and I am lucky to consider close friends: Hugo Tagholm, Pete Lewis, Tom Kay, Lawrence Stafford, Paul Fluin, Bro Diplock, Al Bendall, Alex Light, Ben Cook, Chris Roberts, Rob Evans, Jeremy, Ange and Simon Andrews. Thank you for the continued support and love.

Thank you to all of our customers at Otter Surfboards, many of whom have become good friends over the years. None of this would have happened without you.

When it comes to my deepest feelings of gratitude though, there is no way that I could have done any of this without the continued love and support of my closest friends and family. To Chris Wooton, who is my right hand man and has helped bring positivity and calmness to the workshop for the past seven years; and Ally and Will, who have always found a way to show me support, kindness and how to laugh about everything. Thank you.

To my Mum, Dad and sister Victoria, who have always been by my side through the highs and lows of life and have often made me feel like I can fly. Thank you.

To my wife Liz, I could not have done any of this without your incredible kindness and love. I only hope I can lift you up as high as you do me.

William, if you ever want a glimpse into your father's mind, this book is for you.

Thank you all, I love you.

Books in the series

Also available

Available in print and digital formats from bookshops, online retailers or via our website: **thedobook.co**

To hear about events and forthcoming titles, you can find us on social media @dobookco, or subscribe to our newsletter